THEN AT 44
Henry F. Zacchini

SHIRES PRESS

4869 Main Street
P.O. Box 2200
Manchester Center, VT 05255
www.northshire.com

Book Design: Andy West Design
Cover Photo: Amelia Glickman

Then at Forty-Four
©2018 Henry Zacchini

ISBN: 978-1-60571-420-2

Building Community, One Book at a Time
A family-owned, independent bookstore
in Manchester Ctr., VT, since 1976 and Saratoga Springs, NY since 2013.
We are committed to excellence in bookselling.
The Northshire Bookstore's mission is to serve as a resource for
information, ideas, and entertainment while honoring the needs
of customers, staff, and community.

Printed in the United States of America

Again, For Rachel

ACKNOWLEDGEMENTS

There are countless people who have helped with the production of this book. To my numerous editors including: Greg Joly, Rachel Glickman, Amelia Glickman, Bob Parks, Andy Smith-Petersen, Quinn Zacchini, Sharon Matzek and Henry L. Zacchini, you all helped to make these poems much better than they were. To Andy West, who did beautiful work designing this book, I think I still owe you from the last one. To Amelia Glickman for the cover photograph. To the memory of Evan Bolivar. To all of my friends and family who helped me along the way and who inspired many of these poems, thank you.

From "THE ABANDONED ONE"

You are, you are perhaps, the man or the woman
or the tenderness that deciphered nothing.
Or perhaps you did not clutch the dark human
firmament, the throbbing star, perhaps
on treading you did not know that from the blind earth
comes forth the ardent day of steps that seek you.

But we shall find ourselves unarmed, pressed
among the mute gifts of the final earth.

– PABLO NERUDA

"CYNICAL CAPITALISTS"

Privatize profit.
Socialize loss.

– DAVID BUDBILL

CONTENTS

- **CAVES** 01
- **LONDON** 03
- **ON THE PLANE** 05
- **FREEDOM** 07
- **HUMAN BATH** 09
- **THE LAST DOG** 11
- **IAN OUT ON THE BLUE** 13
- **FASCISTS** (ADVICE FOR A FRIEND) 15
- **GOD IS DARK MATTER** 17
- **ENGLAND v PERU** 19
- **INVERNESS** 21
- **THE BARBER AND FIFTY-FOUR** 23
- **ON THE SPINE OF GOOD HOUSEKEEPING** 25
- **LEST WE FORGET** 27
- **148 AND 2** 29
- **BILLY TWELVETREES** 31
- **BLACK** 33
- **BUGS** 35
- **WRITE POETRY, CHILDREN** 37
- **PARK RANGER PLANTATION TOUR** 39
- **WITH FORCE** 41
- **THE WALL** 43

BUSKING	45
SICK	47
STILL	49
SYMPHONY	51
TEMPLES OF PEACE AND LOVE	53
THE DYING BIRD	55
AN ODE TO CARDENAS	57
THE CANAL	59
FRA ANGELICO	61
COLOR	63
DAO AND CAPITAL	65
THIRTEEN	67
ANOTHER DRUNK	69
WEALTH MANAGEMENT *(REWRITTEN MAGAZINE AD COPY)*	71
TOBIN BRIDGE ELEGY	73
GATES	75
THE BARBER'S BLADE	77
THE EQUINOX	79
SAWZALL	81
BREAKFAST	83
Q & K	85
CHARGED WITH MEETING	87
THE STORM	89
THE GODS OF NEW YORK	91

CAVES

In these caves, in the sinew of the unrelenting suburbs,
soft sucking and blowing pushes lungs,
slowly, gently.
The sacred air presses against tiny sacs buried deep in the chest,
housing the silent, muted breathing of the sleeping dead.

As you rest, the earth plunges on,
in concert with the blood pulsing through your skulls,
just as you floated in the womb,
innocent, without longing, sterile.

Streaking around the fire-breathing sun,
you are fixed to the planet by relentless gravity,
a force stronger than your dreams,
stronger than your human dollhouse,
rooting you to your bed, just shy of crushing bones.

LONDON

Into the magnetic core we come,
ordered to waste,
metal upon metal, smoking and stacked.

Capital call us to the womb.
Stashed in secret clubs and forbidden to mortal men.
Wires connected to wires,
trading what is not theirs
and is not there.

Bow down and serve,
compelled to be devoured.
Everything consumed.

ON THE PLANE

That's the city outside,
serene, beautiful, lights sparkling, beckoning,
burning like embers in a sea of dark ink.

And me,
in this hurtling tube of humanity,
streaking through the frozen air unbidden,
pushing molecules unmoved by my suffering.
I am far from Zen.
My fight or flight mind focused
on what could be and not what is.

Unsettled,
on the edge of panic,
with every flex of the wing
I'm rudely reminded of my inconsequence.

The pilot's voice echoes over muffled speakers.
Thank god.
It's the soothing, rhythmic cadence
of the British moneyed class.
Slowly, deliberately, he tells us where we've been,
where we're going,
what will be.

Does he speak the truth?
Is it a lovely night in London?
Will we arrive unbroken?

Still at this moment we're alive.
Heathen or believer it's a miracle.

FREEDOM

The birds that take flight don't care.
They fly in lines or in circles,
always up in the vanishing sky.

But what can you do
with your forlorn and melancholy soul,
tied to this earth and all its troubles?

Speak of freedom to the birds?
It's not necessary;
they simply fly.

Human freedom is hollow.
Just a desire to escape
the insanity that plagues our race,
nothing more.

Where are the insane birds?

HUMAN BATH

I
The rumours must be confirmed; the tourists need to know.
Is it true there are lines of sandstone buildings
marching down the hills in lovely, uniform rows?

II
The tourist books whisper of the hordes.
But you must, with your own eyes, see the multitudes
wandering in the way of themselves, manoeuvring,
plodding aimlessly with loved ones in tow, milling about
with zombie-weary feet.

III
For a soundtrack the tourists demand insipid music,
so its Bathonian practitioners spread like margarine
through the five central blocks. They blow on little pan flutes,
plugged into karaoke machines.

IV
We see a local homeless man reach his limit, ranting,
pleading with the Simon and Garfunkel parrots to be silent,
presumably to hear himself think.

His outburst is an affront to the agreed upon tourist-as-cow ritual.
People get uneasy. I say put him on the brochure!

V
Sites for our expanded ubiquity, massed beyond reason.
Come Japan, come China, come America, we can now
head home and tell them what we saw!

THE LAST DOG

The last dog died today. When they got him at the pound the man had said, "Ugly and ain't worth a damn, I can tell."

All in all, pretty true. Smallish, with bad eyes, a spiky, rough coat, an unwanted mutt with a predilection for rolling in shit and an incessant yap that drove the man crazy.

Still, they got old and senile and useless together shuffling around the derelict house. No one noticed or cared what they were up to and they didn't give two shits about what anyone else was up to. Bad hips, bad knees, nothing much to do but wait until it was worse and the accretions of age pulled them closer to the earth.

His wife called it "Fred." He ignored her and called it "Dirtbag" or just "Dirt."

Now, "Dirt" the dog was dead. Of who knows what, he was ancient like the man. He just stopped barking and fell over in the front yard.

He had him in a plastic bag in front of the stoop looking up at his wife staring down teary-eyed, protected from death by the screen door.

"Watcha gonna do with him, with Fred?"

"He's goin' in a hole out back." The old man mumbled as he hobbled away. She always asked the same thing when they died. "If you dig that hole, you'll be fallin' in right after."

She wouldn't come out to watch, to scold him further. She never could stand the sight of death.

And he couldn't stand the idea of her watching him bury the last dog.

IAN OUT ON THE BLUE

You goddamn mensch,
with your ramshackle home,
beset with projects never finished and debts never to be paid.

High on the hardscrabble ridge donkeys parade
with ducks and cats and dogs,
puttering around the place in concert with their master,
heedless of the world below.

With your used hands,
you work the land on a piece of this tragic island,
a place ransacked by your countryman.
But, if you are the new breed of Englishman,
then there is hope for redemption,
more should come.

Because, you want no bloody conquest, no sea of riches,
no enslaved masses.

You want friendship, orchards, community,
and to dig into the consecrated earth
with others like-minded or willing.

The bankers own your ass, but I wish for you the last laugh,
loping along the top of this hill with empty pockets and a full heart.

FASCISTS *(ADVICE FOR A FRIEND)*

Don't
jump when there's a bump in the night,
you don't have to.
When talking heads implore you
to hate, to vengeance,
realize they have small minds.
They are fed lies about strength through unity
that are fed to you.

You think of safety,
of protection,
of what's dear to you;
they think nothing of the sort.
Killing or maiming
is sport,
to quench their predatory need,
for power,
for wealth.

You see,
your needs are not their needs:
they kill whether you like it or not.

You think
if our fascists kill their fascists,
all will be well.
But,
children will grow up fatherless and impoverished,
and some will seek revenge.
Should they question their fathers' right to life?

CONTINUED...

What do you owe your children
and generations yet unborn?
We know that war feeds war
and hatred breeds hatred.

Is this the inheritance
you want spawned?

Must our grace go unspoken?
Are we doomed to kill without mercy?

GOD IS DARK MATTER

Blinding in its infinity, core barren as the heart of the sun,
eternities darker than the void in your dreaming skull,
it binds the multiverse with ineffable power.

God is not starlight, not your eyes squinting in the sun.
God is pure blackness to endless measure.

You will not be drawn into the light,
but into the dark,
from where you came.

ENGLAND v PERU

Oh, come teeming hordes,
raise your glasses and bellow at the top of your lungs.

Scream. Scream for your fathers and grandfathers
who never had a fighting chance other than to spill blood.

Teeter into the sacred coliseum.
Rise as shadows, ghosts of lost empire.

Empire brought the colonized to your door but here you can forget.
You are with your Viking brethren.

Denuded now, you will gain nothing beyond
the false hope of new conquests
and the covenant of patriotic songs.

For two hours, bawl. Lay out your beating, bleating hearts.

Stagger out victorious. Sway with the drunken throng.
Vomit, roll on the ground: laugh, fight, sleep.

Tomorrow will come without absolution.

INVERNESS

It's so far north here; there is nothing beyond but cold earth
where time is measured in ice,
where humanity, even in its colossal abundance,
has not seen fit to settle.

Laid out without purpose or intention,
superimposed over a place that was real.

Bring your bodies to bear under the sullen, constant grey sky.
Carry your shopping waste among your fellows,
breathe in the cold autumn air.

Under the rain, under the low northern sun,
the promise of wealth, of warmer days,
fleeting as your misspent youth.

But on this border, far from the diaspora,
the light plays tricks and the sky fills with rainbows after the deluge.

Are they enough to keep your restless hearts at bay?

THE BARBER AND FIFTY-FOUR

His mind drifts elsewhere but the detail is in his work.
He sculpts my middle age mop with deft precision
born of endless repetition.

"You know that fellow Joe?" the elderly customer asks,
placing his testimonial-come-question in the middle
of a Saturday request for a Wednesday slot.

The barber mumbles a reply, noncommittal
as he works on my head.

"Joe," the man insists gently, "you know, the bloke
from down the road with cancer, it turns out it's really serious."

The barber's face is unchanged, worn, sagging,
and slightly morose.

The man made his appointment
but hesitated, hoping to close the loop.
One last try, "He's only 54."

"Oh, that's too bad," the barber says, almost to himself.
The concerned patron shuffles to the door.

The barber takes me to the washtub. He scrubs with aggression.
Is this normal English barbershop conduct?

In the waiting area, a balding man with uncertain hair cutting
needs asks the barber if he's heard about the motorcyclist.

CONTINUED...

"Yes, I read about it," the barber replies quietly, not looking up from
my head. The customer says the motorcyclist was a neighbour.

Close now, the action is delicate,
with hands working electric clippers and comb.

"His son was coming over for a visit then he saw
his dad's bike in the road so he stopped.
He'd hit the car in front, went sprawling, lived through that one
but the car coming the other way got him. Only 54. Poor chap."

With a quick sideways glance the barber mutters an answer,
"Oh that's terrible," he says, while he finishes his cuts.

He offers his first smile when we're done,
perhaps just happy he can move on to the next head.
He makes a joke I don't catch, we both laugh.

I trudge home with my shortened, greying hairs;
a step closer to one end than the other.

ON THE SPINE OF GOOD HOUSEKEEPING

I. JANUARY 2014
Washer Dryers: Death, Bondage, Lies
Cream Liqueurs: Faded Dreams, Hangover, Cheap Date
Anti-Aging Beauty: Ants Eat Your Body
Cereal Bars: Not Real Food

II. FEBRUARY 2014
Prosecco: See Cream Liqueurs Above
Croissants: You'll Never Make These
Soup Makers: Hot Better Than Cold
Slow Cookers: Into the Abyss
Blenders: Add Two Roaches to Your Smoothie for Protein

III. MARCH 2014
Washing Machines: The World is Unclean
Tumble Dryers: See Washer Dryers Above
Irons: See Slow Cookers Above
Red Roses: False Promises, Columbian Slaves

LEST WE FORGET

Fall in line.

You wear the red flower of remembrance
not for the betrayed dead,
but for you.

Politicians approach the war statue with bowed heads,
with false reverence, with wreaths in their hands
and death in their hearts.

Oceans of sweet crimson poppies turned into vigils
for the senseless butchery.
The poor poppy, so abused and forsaken.

Children in uniforms saluting the cameras in that sea of red:
used for shameful, scandalous ends.

What should be a warning, a call to peace,
reduced to reflexive pantomime.

Lest we forget who ordered the slaughter.
Lest we forget it was you.

148 AND 2

What would the mystics say about this calamity, the Buddhists?

That life is an unanswerable question.
That only love can trump ignorance.
That life is an illusion.
That the only relief is to succour grief with compassion.

And yet, as years turn to generations and generations to centuries,
the swell of the living's unimaginable sorrow will disappear
until all is forgotten.

And when existence grinds to an end
and our gods hear nary a whisper
over the monotonous wind as it caresses the relentless frozen earth,
who will mourn when the last cell, mired in depths beyond light,
ceases to be?

BILLY TWELVETREES

Have you seen the man they call Billy Twelvetrees
with long golden hair and blood on his knees?
The fanatics go mad when he leaps for the ball,
kicking and screaming and stamping them all.

A youth unearthly in strength and in speed
boys on the playground had to take heed.
His childhood rivals left him alone
lest he stomp on their precious little boy bones.

Now a mop top blond beast of a man,
he makes hay crunching a ball in his hands.
Men cry out loud on account of his feats
his smile and muscles make young housewives weep.

Do it Twelvetrees, Welsh and Froggies be damned,
reach for that touch, pummel them low,
hunt them down wherever they go.
It's never too late to run a little amuck
as the men from abroad are battered and struck.

Billy knows it's a game, but he plays to win,
down in that scrum, skin bashing skin.
For England, for country, for Vikings of men,
bruised and battered, he fights to the end!

Twelvetrees, Twelvetrees, a song of a name,
a near perfect fit for this bloody old game.

BLACK

Come, pile in like ewes for slaughter,
turned, tweaked and twisted into forms altogether human.

These packaged goods,
this incarcerated madness
fed by slaves on the sixteen-hour line.

We are betrayed.
Blinded,
by consumption, by greed,
we forgot we'll die.

How can we reconcile, beyond possession and acquisition,
the longing and loneliness of our meretricious hearts?

BUGS

You and all your fucking, flying friends crave the artificial light.
You're primeval and you want in.

What will you do if you get here?
You'll buzz around the lights in endless circles
until your crazy little wings and hearts stop beating.

You have the whole night to explore.
Do it while you still can.
The lights keep us from dreaming.

WRITE POETRY, CHILDREN

Come children, now we'll write poetry.
Forget spelling and grammar and science and math.

Have no concern for the drilling of hard facts into your skulls.
(Here's an adult secret: school will eat your soul.)

No need to ready you for exploiting or to be exploited.
Today we will compose odes to love, to beauty,
to flowers, to play, to friendship.

Onwards, follow your hearts!

That's correct Timmy, you can write.
You can turn your feelings into words that sing.

This lovely blue earth-our host-is alive and beckons us to live,
to share our collective experience.

Put away that nonsense for a day and we'll roll in the mud,
we'll sing like birds. We'll swim in the river
and let it carry us gently away.

Pay no heed to order or form, just put it down,
scratch it out, bellow from inside.

Today we will write because our hearts beat,
because for this fleeting moment, defying odds beyond reason,
we are alive.

PARK RANGER PLANTATION TOUR

Angela's is not the sanitized tour.
This is not the edited-for-convenience
Monticello and Mount Vernon show,
"There was some enslavement, true,
but isn't this home lovely?"

Day by day, on this execrable ground,
unshackling minds from generational lies,
she digs through the attic uncovering shackles,
chains, whips and spiked collars.

Children pursued, tortured, murdered.
Women, men, the elderly,
violated without conscience to enrich the few.
America's spine was built this way.

Speak the truth Angela. The country's wealth came from theft
and theft alone: of dignity, humanity, family, blood, labor and love.

The wealth is with the descendants of the thieves.

Who will repay? Who will repossess?

WITH FORCE

To choose between peace and love this is not.
Presented as a choice of good versus evil,
it's an enchanting and spellbinding scheme.

The peddlers of death always show their hand.
They kill innocents without reservation,
they poison wells without conscience.

From sharp-toothed jaws flapping in time
with their ventriloquist's hand, the maleficent mouths
of the marketers spew a fiction about humanitarian missions.

For generations, for profit, they march forward; armies protecting
elite interests, everything else is inconsequential fodder.

Now the beheading Satan's spawn has come to lay waste.

Lies upon lies built like cages against mercy; murderers all,
professing their sacred cause, killing until killing
becomes the righteous path.

Choose sides or be called a heretic.
Choose sides or be labelled an enemy.
Reject both and realize you've been trapped inside the asylum.

THE WALL

The imperfect stone wall, so beautiful,
lovingly made with expert hands and passion,
topped with a dollop of cement for endurance
to withstand the earth's vocal impermanence.

Just beyond, a bramble, a thicket, an unwelcome place.
Hot and wet with life, filled with bugs and plants that bite.

The sky, so beautiful, rife with planets and stars.
The minutia and the grandiose coexist in equal, endless measure.

Beyond the sky, blackness, eternity,
calling us ever back to the beginning,
before time, before existence, to benign chaos,
to the infinity which orders all and makes us whole.

BUSKING

Mulcahey sings on the corner of a random street in Ireland
with his crumpled dime store coat and mussed hair.

Large and gangly, even in his middle age:
boyish, youthful, as if he's still not clear
how his limbs are put together.

The lyrics funny, poignant, about love and fragile hearts.
He looks to the passers-by as he sings to them.
Most don't look back.
Of course, the children look.

Heedless, voice rising and falling sweetly,
he pauses to hold the car door for a nun and receives a thank you.
Finishing with a flourish, he gently touches his fellow player's arm.

In this luckless world we have music to accompany the unravelling.

SICK

The rulers and owners never tire of war;
it feeds their desolate souls.
Hatred and profit order their lives.

To live is to spill blood;
to make lackeys kill,
to convince each and all,
murder is the cure for our troubles.
Brutally wearying,
stripping mental faculties,
denuding hope for humanity.

Being farmers of death,
they plant seeds of malice.
They lie-
know they lie.

Youth, come in your blindness,
offer hope and protection before middle age unearths,
in full relief,
the terminal terror of war.

Because we sleep,
knowing what's done,
is done in our name.

STILL

Still the beast's mechanical beating heart drones into the ears
and into the gut, unrelenting, existence be damned,
the harbinger of civilization's end.

In quiet, long-tamed forests on this settled island
there are days when nothing moves,
when the creature is hushed enough to be just out of reach,
days with stillness unmatched.

Not a flower spurned by an unsheltered bee, not a primordial fern
waving its maniacal windblown greeting,
not a woman's whispered confession of love taken on the wind.
Everything still.

Did not the stillness lead to madness,
to a pillage that made Rome's maiden blush?
They hollowed out and possessed the world.

Are your eyes blinded?
Can you see your place now in the world?
Can you grasp the wreckage spawned by your ruling caste?

SYMPHONY

The symphony started again this morning.
Right outside our window overlooking the forest.
It began with those birds that I cannot name
whose two-tone call goes
high-low, high-low, high-low.

Then slowly, like a whisper, the rain began to fall
and the birds and I sat up to listen.

When I clumsily lay back down my wife is annoyed.
"Shush," she says. "You're like a bull in a China shop."

TEMPLES OF PEACE AND LOVE

Consider the wealth, the grandeur, the priceless works of art,
the impossibility of constructing these buildings over generations,
requiring funds beyond reason.

Can we imagine Christ in his dirty robes,
broken sandals and dark skin welcomed here?

Generals from conquering Christian armies and holy marauding
saints are revered with statues. Devils incarnate who required that
the impoverished, heathen natives worship the white man's god.

Let us look at the massive triumphant statue of Saint James in the
Granada Cathedral, sword raised in victory, horse trampling
a prostrate Muslim apostate. "IN CHIRST'S NAME REJOICE!"

The Reconquista is complete, the Catholic Monarchs return;
all that remains undone are the bloody inquisition at home
and the exploitation and genocide of the Indians.

Now imagine the Christ (manifest in a second coming)
arriving in Spain.
He is taken to the Granada Cathedral,
his flock wanting to show him the glory of what they've erected
to profess their love. They lead him into the church with growing
throngs following close on his heels.

He enters with the multitude.
The beauty overwhelms him.
The crowd swells.
He pauses to look at the statue of Saint James.

CONTINUED...

He stands rooted, staring.
In his frailty, in his colossal humanness, he weeps.

He throws himself on the ground and begs for god's forgiveness
on behalf of his human acolytes.

At the sight of their god's sorrow, the worshippers wail
and howl and pull their hair in anguish.

After long prayers of atonement, he rises and goes
from one penitent to the next, lifting them up,
whispering his love as he kisses their tear-splattered faces.

THE DYING BIRD

My child and I walked home after spending a day together
as wayfaring strangers. We ran across a dying pigeon
rooted to the sidewalk.

I noticed it the moment before she did
and began to steel myself for what was to come.

"Oh, look at that pigeon, I think it's got a broken wing and can't fly."
She wanted to stop. She wanted to help it.

I walked on hoping she'd follow me.
When I was a child I would have wanted to stop too.
Having seen more death and suffering, we pretend we're tough.

"Come on honey, there's nothing we can do. A cat will eat it."
Was that the best I could do, "A cat will eat it?"

The truth is that part of me wanted to help too.
The bird was beautiful, helpless and suffering.

I tried a different tack. "Maybe it's just sick and needs a rest."

"Yes," she said. "Maybe it will get better and fly away."

We walked towards home not speaking,
alienated in this world and ignorant of the next.

AN ODE TO CARDENAS

When the foreign oil barons reigned, taking all profits with them
and leaving scraps for the people, you sent them into exile.

They cried like angry babes in a playpen,
"The oil is ours, you have no right to take it from us." But you did.

They got their big brothers to threaten you,
to make you give up the oil. They said you'd stolen from them.

That was a lifetime ago, but the men who run oil for profit
have long memories and the dirty dollar
makes their wanton minds blind with greed.

They worked through generations to end their exile,
to make what was never theirs, theirs again. They needed help.

They needed a president who was unlike you in every way:
a coward, a tool, a pretty mask, an enemy of the people.

They finally found their man.

THE CANAL

This bestial place.
This plasticized world, strewn with waste.

A refuge for the strung out,
the addicted,
the homeless,
the dissolute
and horn-dog teenagers.

Lined with lumbering, crumbling industry,
newly assembled ant-dwellings
and skinny canal boats spewing fumes for heat.

Bedecked with yuppies huffing and puffing in kayaks
and muck-splattered white swans paddling
around discarded packaging, we cycle beside this lunacy.

We plunge our bikes through the sludge under hostile winter skies.
You say you can't go on, through the refuse, through the mud.
The dirty swans are the final affront;
you apply the brakes and refuse to roll.

So we return, passing under multifold, anonymous canal bridges
distinct only by their numbered placards-128, 130, 132, 134, 136,
all leading from one godforsaken place to the next.

FRA ANGELICO

Day after pitiless day under the watchful eyes of a merciless god,
walking empty, stone-hewn hallways ever towards their sinful doom,
if only the monks could express their love for the Christ forsaken.

Brothers' shoes wear away the floor,
year after year, amplifying stones,
breaking the silence of passages at odds with noise.
Padded feet become the symphony and street noises
the cacophony for the monks in their rooms.

Some brothers dream of god's golden fields, of verdant forests
teeming with life, but they are here, in the city,
surrounded by prostitutes and thieves,
by rich men lording their wealth,
by motherless children begging in the streets,
by the teeming mass of wayward sinners
looking for meaning in the world,
searching for a crumb to eat and a place to rest.

In this human gully with nothing but time and prayer to fill the days,
how to forestall the creeping madness?
By walls covered with angels and demons for the living world.

He painted the hallways, so that steps between rooms
were shrouded in consecration.

Yet faith enshrined was not close enough.
The hallways were collective tracks,
the brothers' private rooms were unwatched,
a place for a god-fearing man to be away from repentance.

CONTINUED...

Portraits were needed to comfort the brothers as they slept, as they shit, as they prayed. Room-by-room, through countless hours and endless days, the paintings took form.

"Yes," the brother said, "the one above me,
must be of the Lord's violated rib.
Show the sacred blood gushing out of him,
reveal how none of the unbelievers heeded
its extraordinary fall to the earth and how Christians did.
Make certain that his face shows the suffering and the glory
of his love. Help me feel his heart as my heart."

In the convent of Saint Mark, the brothers saw beauty
through the eyes of the master.

COLOR

Is there color between the stars,
inside your heart,
amidst the sinew of your muscles,
between the cells of your blood,
in the entrails of your nerves?

Riot of life, bastard of the sun.
Burn my eyes with your glory,
with your spite of blind infinity.

In the chasm of my brain thoughts get stuck on black,
at times without will,
as it fires with accidental purpose.

These hues keep us from heartless gravity,
from battered nothingness.
Living blindly on the margin of universes untamed,
we long for relief from the enveloping blackness.

DAO AND CAPITAL

*Therefore the place of what is firm and strong is below,
and that of what is soft and weak is above.* – LAO TSE

*The sage does not accumulate (for himself). The more that he
expends for others, the more does he possess of his own; the more
that he gives to others, the more does he have himself.* – LAO TSE

They take anything and misuse it.
They take the name of an ancient creed
of brotherhood and balance, and blaspheme it
to justify their greed,
their pillage.

The high priests of capitalism write books
equating the glories of exploitation with great spiritual teachings.
To them this makes sense. Conquerors always take sense
in their madness.

They are the boy bully destroyers of the sand castle.
A swift kick here, a bashing there, now wrecked.
The maker's eyes wet with tears.
The destroyer's face illuminated with joy.

Of course, the day will come when the merrymaking ends:
maybe tomorrow, maybe in five hundred years.
When it does, the masters' progeny will suffer with the rest.

They sicken the earth and each other; they kill for power;
they enrich the few and impoverish the many.
Our sycophant leaders say the reason

CONTINUED...

for such suffering and disuse is that we've not allowed enough
greed and self-concern to enter our lives.
Still, the great teachers saw
what the capitalists and their servants will never see:
that our reason for being is to organize against this sacrilege
and to glorify what's left of the beautiful earth.

THIRTEEN

How to express the ineffable, unspoken beating of my heart?
My beautiful daughter, how can I record my selfish feelings?

Everything is fragile, flashing quickly in the light.
As the world spins relentlessly through the void
we cling fast to its outermost edges.

Yes, it's true:
we are preposterously here and in abundance beyond measure.
Still you shine in my eyes.

We are all betrothed to the earth and what's in it.
Can you feel your place?
Will you care for the unloved when given the chance?

My bias is my delusion.
I love you.

ANOTHER DRUNK

For a year or more we talked, in trifles,
across the garden fence.
Separated by years, by birth,
by black oceans.

Living out our middling lives.
You, sensing the end is close,
me pretending it's far.

I tempt you inside.
Together in my home,
we are in forbidden space.

We begin the talk inside.
Weather or cars,
suburban banality,
a poor stage for review.

Your wife told a secret
-you're a drunk.
The doctor said:
a bit more of it
and you'll be dead.

It gets you early or late, I know.
The sickness.
The guilt, the resentment, the anger,
powerless over our destructive obsession.

CONTINUED...

What's been lost?
Have you been wandering in the night
through your dark kitchen,
craving?

Now, let us speak of forgiveness, love.

WEALTH MANAGEMENT
(REWRITTEN MAGAZINE AD COPY)

"We may not be right for you."
Dispossessed, black, out of work,
no assets, detained,
imprisoned, near enslavement,
we may not be right for you.

Poor white trash like your daddy,
nothing to hope for,
taught to hate others impoverished.
Fucked without asking to be.
"We may not be right for you."

Rich, handed leisure without effort.
Sated, but not content with your one-percent life?
Want to crawl on the heads of your brethren?
"We may be right for you."

Let's get to it.
"Minimum relationship ten million dollars."

TOBIN BRIDGE ELEGY

I.
When you were small and sparkling the bridge was wondrous.
The largest you'd ever seen and,
like you, young and resplendent.

II.
Your mother and father up front
as the car barrels toward the bridge.
You with your sisters in the back,
teasing them to get a rise.

You play, as a child plays, unknowing.
The old car climbs onto the bridge
and your father sends up a small warning shot.
"Hey, quiet down back there."
You don't know it's the only chance you'll get.

The car is now high above the lazy, broad river.
You continue teasing,
but the car has stopped. The moment has arrived;
you see it on his face as he turns to you.
Helplessness and alcoholism and fury animate his reddened, insane face.

You flinch back instinctively groping for one of your sisters,
hoping to hold on to them, but they are also afraid.

"Goddamn you, I told you to shut up!"
He gets out of the car and reaches for your door.
A sickening horror rises in your gut.

CONTINUED...

"Do you want me to throw you off this goddamn bridge?"
The door is open; you are at his mercy.

You plead, "I didn't mean it, I'm sorry."

Your mother yells something unintelligible from the front seat
but you can't hear over your pounding heart.
Your sisters are dead silent, tears blur your eyes.
Leaning away from him you beg, "Please!"
He grabs you and drags you to the edge.

III.
Today we're driving over the same bridge stuck in traffic with my
children in tow and your rage is palpable.

"Fucking cops, they've gotta have something better to do with their
time than holding up all this traffic. They must enjoy this, getting off
on their power."

I feel the rage: it comes easily.
But what can I say?
How can I push back against generational madness?

You tell me later that there was a jumper on the bridge.
The cops were attempting to save a life.

IV.
The bridge, finely balanced between two irreconcilable shores,
offers no pleas or supplications.
It is, as it was, unmoved.

GATES

We match gaits, you just ahead.
We are: countless times together on the trodden path.
Feet born to the earth,
old knees protest.
Just the start and the least of the
ill at ease march up the mountain.

Our marriage in a squall
no lovers' walk,
but one to air grievances,
to clarify points.

To begin the fray; a hidden logistics salvo
concerning production of the evening meal.
That's as far as we get to normal.
With all the death and misery,
on the human earth
we add, to what end,
to the toll.
As our bodies work
we troll.

To the top and down again.
Resentments, misunderstandings,
forces set upon us
upon our union
like beating dust from the tattered rug
stitched by love,
worn, still beautiful,
ours.

CONTINUED...

Near the bottom now, almost running
late for god knows what.
My take-out suggestion will not stand.
We settle on noodles.

THE BARBER'S BLADE

The barber's blade,
as it scratches away the flesh and hair on my neck
is in a fine state of balance.
The blade, the barber and I have a small compact.

A touch more pressure,
a nick and a bit of blood is spilled.

"You felt that when I nicked you," she says coolly.

She has proven to have nimble, expert hands.
Maybe some nicks are meant to be.
Maybe the blood helps sort through the monotony of days,
just a few drops to distill the blade's possible resolve.

For cordiality's sake, I don't mind sparing a little.

THE EQUINOX

The earth and everything in it forced still to serve you.
In the unending days of your preeminence,
you wander the earth,
wondering why you must die.
It's true that your prayers to the god created in your image
are no longer needed.

To the columned houses built on blood,
to the sanctified weddings, enshrined here,
married to material well-being.
All the people in the brochures smiling at their dumb luck.

The valley filled with stores of shit
scrubbed for your vision of a hygienic world.
Golf, Land Rover mud tours and fly-fishing order creation.
Quiet, peaceful activities where,
as your mind wanders,
you can think of your bank account,
of your property, of your safety,
of a country arranged for your security,
with slavery offshored for convenience.

This fucking white-washed world.
When will the madness end?
Too long has it mastered humanity,
too long has it sucked at the marrow of every living thing.
If they are done with their prayers, then let us begin.
Let us pray for systemic death
bred from a thousand cuts, richly earned.

SAWZALL

I came today with the quivering fire of the Sawzall
to attack the rotten post.
It's a nasty machine with a floppy jagged blade
that cuts,
but not straight.

The ants, I know, saw the post differently.
That wet rotten wood was the place to tunnel,
to protect their queen mother,
to hide her white maggot eggs from hungry birds.

A few bit my flesh as I cut, pried, and hammered,
but most fled, some running pell-mell,
others carrying eggs as they went.
If this were a badger's den or bird's nest
I may have harbored doubts,
but I would accept no ant excuse
for trying to make my house theirs.

BREAKFAST

Into the window the bird comes,
glowing, wings pumping time, pushing air,
awake for hours now and loosed from the bonds of gravity.

I sit with you for breakfast, awake for minutes.
Minds stunted by the coming light,
eyes sensitive to the sun,
thoughts jumbled,
conversation untrammeled by wit or imagination.

Hunger and a dull headache fill the void.
Perfunctory words sluggishly stir our listless minds.

Like the bell of the master,
the sound of the bird striking the glass door pulls us from our stupor.
On the deck its spindly legs gently retract.
A thing of beauty, inert.

That instant, that moment,
from the yes to the no,
an admirable aerial acrobat now fallen,
open beak no longer in need of fresh air, just a coin for Charon.

Like us the birds dream.
Tucked into its nest the bird dreamt through the cloudless night
and its dreams were as unknowable as the meaning of the world.

Q & K

At night you and the forest enclose me.
I am not angry with the trees for their hushed watching
for their battle scars and seeming indifference to the lives we lead.
They are long-lived and must too bear the wrath
of storms unbidden.

You built that stone wall and it partially surrounds me.
To die so young while I'm still here.
Yet, I think of you not just at night but in the spring.
When the leaves come out they are young,
immodest, wet with life,
how I remember you.

CHARGED WITH MEETING

What if instead we held the meeting
next to that little brook
and all looked for a small underwater stone to share
and took it in hand
and passed it around
and saw its luminosity
and noted how the water
for centuries
had brushed its stubborn
naked facade
and how it lay there
patient beyond measure,
undeterred.

Then, done with our sightseeing,
we walked back inside
the brushed concrete walls
discharged and refreshed
to turn our minds and cars towards home.

THE STORM

we weathered the storm
as we slept
the mighty trees swayed
as metal turned to rust
as the brook, once docile,
flowed mean near its banks
while the old wooden play box shelter
hardly moved
and our dreams, such as they were,
held fast to projecting the jittery camera version of our lives
electrical impulses
falling
in and out of the void
less of a thing than the hundred million raindrops
which fell to the earth
unabashed and with abandon

THE GODS OF NEW YORK

When the gods come from New York to play,
blowing and beating their instruments in the swelter
strong enough
they vibrate the soda can's skin,

and as the cold comes slowly,
the crickets speak with lower voices
and they die with little time
as the late summer heat sticks to bones without mercy

you walk out of the house weeping,
onto the dirt road, through the forest, into the dark
dragging along depths of grief I can't repair
sad for the kids, for the lost dog you loved,
for the emptiness which stalks our days.

I will drive down our road, to pick you up as you asked,
I will listen and talk softly of things you may not hear,
I am with you,
your lover
and I will take you to see the gods of New York.